FASTEST ANIMALS

That's Wild!
A Look at Animals

Julie Murray

ABDO Publishing Company

VISIT US AT
www.abdopublishing.com

Published by ABDO Publishing Company, 8000 West 78th Street, Edina, Minnesota 55439.

Copyright © 2010 by Abdo Consulting Group, Inc. International copyrights reserved in all countries. No part of this book may be reproduced in any form without written permission from the publisher. Buddy Books™ is a trademark and logo of ABDO Publishing Company.

Printed in the United States of America, North Mankato, Minnesota.
112009
012010

 PRINTED ON RECYCLED PAPER

Coordinating Series Editor: Rochelle Baltzer
Editor: Sarah Tieck
Contributing Editors: Heidi M.D. Elston, Megan M. Gunderson, BreAnn Rumsch, Marcia Zappa
Graphic Design: Deborah Coldiron, Maria Hosley
Cover Photograph: *Eighth Street Studio*; *iStockphoto*: ©iStockphoto/Rouzes; *Peter Arnold, Inc.*: Martin Harvey.
Interior Photographs/Illustrations: *Amazing Creatures CD*: Stockbyte (pp. 5, 29); *AnimalsAnimals - Earth Scenes*: Alan G. Nelson (p. 8); *Brandon Cole Marine Photography*: Brandon Cole (pp. 5, 21, 23, 25); *Eighth Street Studio* (pp. 12, 15, 16, 30); *iStockphoto*: ©iStockphoto/ (p. 19), ©iStockphoto/agencyby (p. 8), ©iStockphoto/ HughStonelan (p. 27), ©iStockphoto/mammamaart (p. 29), ©iStockphoto/morgan (p. 29), ©iStockphoto/ photosfromafrica (p. 15); *Peter Arnold, Inc.*: ©Biosphoto/Cavignaux Régis (p. 27), X. Eichaker (p. 11), S.J. Krasemann (p. 5), WILDLIFE (p. 15); *Photos.com* (p. 23); *Shutterstock*: Bryant Aardema (p. 7), Mudasser Ahmeddar (p. 7), Mircea Bezergheanu (p. 7), Sascha Burkard (p. 19), Steve Byland (p. 13), Ronnie Howard (p. 5), iDesign (p. 13), Petr Jilek (p. 11), Marie Lumiere (p. 17), Morgan Lane Photography (p. 29), Arthur Eugene Preston (p. 23).

Library of Congress Cataloging-in-Publication Data

Murray, Julie, 1969-
Fastest animals / Julie Murray.
p. cm. -- (That's wild! : a look at animals)
ISBN 978-1-60453-978-3
1. Animal locomotion--Juvenile literature. 2. Speed--Juvenile literature. I. Title.
QP301.M74 2009
590--dc22
2009033007

Contents

Wildly Fast!

Pronghorn

Many amazing animals live in our world. Some are big and others are small. They may fly, run, or swim.

Some animals are wildly fast! Their bodies are built to move quickly. Speed helps animals catch meals, avoid danger, or survive in their **habitats**. Let's learn more about fast animals!

Pacific Ocean

Killer Whale

4

Fast animals live all over the world. The same type of animal may live in several parts of the world.

Peregrine Falcon

Cheetahs

North America

Europe

Asia

Africa

South America

Australia

Antarctica

Atlantic Ocean

Pacific Ocean

Indian Ocean

Southern Ocean

5

Fastest Flyers

Fast birds often have lightweight bodies. They use their strong chest **muscles** to flap their long wings. Their body shape helps them move easily through the air.

Birds fly at different speeds depending on the situation. Some fly very fast when they are scared. Others fly fast when they dive to catch **prey**. Wind can change the speed of birds, too.

Birds use their wings to change direction and control speed.

8

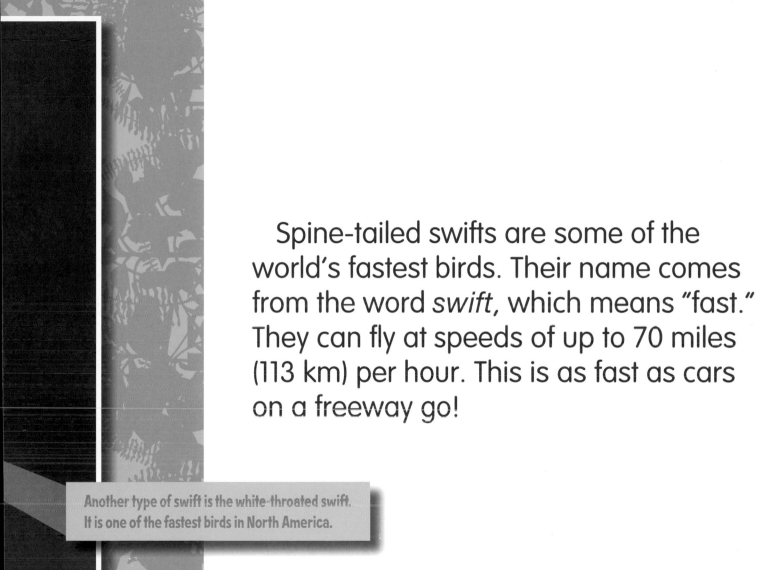

Spine-tailed swifts are some of the world's fastest birds. Their name comes from the word *swift*, which means "fast." They can fly at speeds of up to 70 miles (113 km) per hour. This is as fast as cars on a freeway go!

Another type of swift is the white-throated swift. It is one of the fastest birds in North America.

9

World's Fastest

The peregrine falcon is not only the world's fastest bird. It is also the world's fastest animal! It can dive at a speed of 200 miles (322 km) per hour! Its regular flying speed is about 50 miles (80 km) per hour.

Peregrine falcons hunt other birds, such as pigeons and ducks. They dive fast and catch **prey** in midair!

Peregrine falcons dive almost straight down. This is called stooping.

Winging It

A hummingbird's wings move so fast that you almost can't see them! Some flap 70 times per second.

These fast-flapping wings help hummingbirds fly quickly. Hummingbirds usually fly about 25 miles (40 km) per hour. When they dive, they can reach speeds of 60 miles (97 km) per hour!

12

Hummingbirds can quickly fly up, down, forward, backward, and sideways.

13

A cheetah's spine bends easily. This helps it move fast.

Speed Racer

Cheetahs are the fastest animals on land. Most live in **grasslands** in Africa. For short distances, cheetahs can run up to 70 miles (113 km) per hour. When these big cats run, it looks like they are flying!

14

Spot the Speeder

A cheetah has two stripes on its face. Each stripe runs from one of its eyes down to its mouth. This is one way people tell it apart from a leopard.

Cheetahs run fast when chasing **prey**. They attack animals such as birds, rabbits, and antelope.

A cheetah's narrow body helps it move fast. Its strong claws **grip** the ground as it runs. And its long tail helps it balance. Even its nose shape helps the cheetah easily breathe when running fast.

The cheetah is famous for its spotted coat.

17

The Long Run

The second-fastest land animal is the pronghorn. It lives in the **grasslands** of North America. Most pronghorn can run about 50 miles (80 km) per hour!

A pronghorn is slower than a cheetah. But, it can run for longer amounts of time. It has a large heart and **lungs**. And, its body is strong enough to handle high speeds.

The pronghorn's eyes are large for its body. This makes it easier to see predators. Then, the pronghorn can make a quick escape!

19

Water Wonders

The fastest fish have smooth, specially shaped bodies. Their body shape helps them move easily through water. They also have strong **muscles** and tails that push them along.

Marlins are one of the fastest fish.

Shortfin mako sharks are among the fastest sharks.

21

The sailfish is the fastest fish in the sea. It can swim about 70 miles (113 km) per hour! Sailfish live far offshore and often **migrate**. These speedy fish are huge. Sailfish can be more than six feet (2 m) long. They can weigh more than 200 pounds (90 kg).

No Way!

Most female sailfish lay more than 4 million eggs at a time.

Sailfish are named for their large fin. It looks like a boat's sail.

23

Hungry Hunter

Not all underwater creatures are fish. One of the fastest water **mammals** is the killer whale.

Killer whales can swim about 30 miles (50 km) per hour. Sometimes, they do flips and jumps while swimming. Their speed helps them catch **prey**, such as salmon.

Male killer whales live about 30 years. Females live about 50 years.

25

Fast Talker

Some animals have just one body part that moves fast. For chameleons, it is their tongue. This creature moves its tongue so fast you can hardly see it!

Chameleons eat bugs. Their quick tongues help them catch dinner, even though their bodies move slowly.

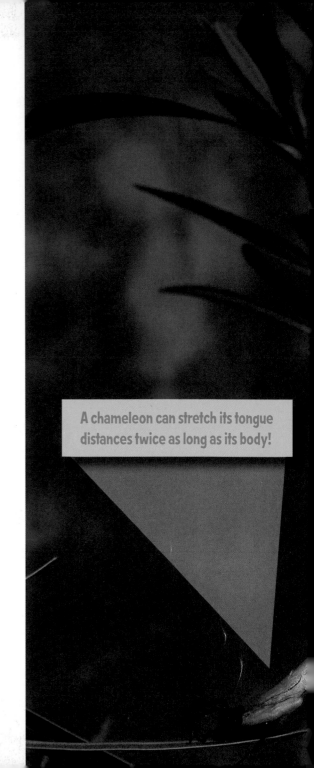

A chameleon can stretch its tongue distances twice as long as its body!

26

Now You See Me, Now You Don't

Chameleons can change their body color to match their surroundings. This special skill helps them hide from predators.

27

That WAS Wild!

From running cheetahs to diving falcons, there are some very fast wild animals. Each of them is an important part of the animal kingdom.

People work hard to **protect** animals and their surroundings. You can help, too! Recycling and using less water are two simple things you can do. The more you learn, the more you can do to help keep animals safe.

28

Planting a tree may provide some wild animals with a home.

Cheetahs are at risk. People hunt them for their unusual fur. And, their grasslands are being turned into farming and building areas.

It is important to reduce, reuse, and recycle. This helps protect wild animal habitats.

29

Wow! Is That TRUE?

🐾 After a fast run to catch prey, cheetahs sometimes need a break. They may have to rest for 20 to 30 minutes. Then, they can eat the prey they caught.

🐾 Greyhounds are some of the fastest dogs. They can reach speeds faster than 40 miles (64 km) per hour. Greyhounds sometimes run in races.

🐾 Turtles are known to move slowly on land. Yet, some can swim almost six miles (10 km) per hour!

Important Words

grassland a large area of grass, with little or no trees.

grip to hold tightly.

habitat a place where a living thing is naturally found.

lungs a body part that helps the body breathe.

mammal a group of living beings. Mammals have hair and make milk to feed their babies.

migrate to move from one place to another to find food or have babies.

muscles (MUH-suhls) body tissues, or layers of cells, that help move the body.

prey an animal hunted or killed by a predator for food.

protect (pruh-TEHKT) to guard against harm or danger.

Web Sites

To learn more about fast animals, visit ABDO Publishing Company online. Web sites about fast animals are featured on our Book Links page. These links are routinely monitored and updated to provide the most current information available.

www.abdopublishing.com

31

Index